Treasures of Nature
Ferns

Photoscreens of Ferns by John Streams

Designed by William Houston

The Crossing Press / Freedom, California

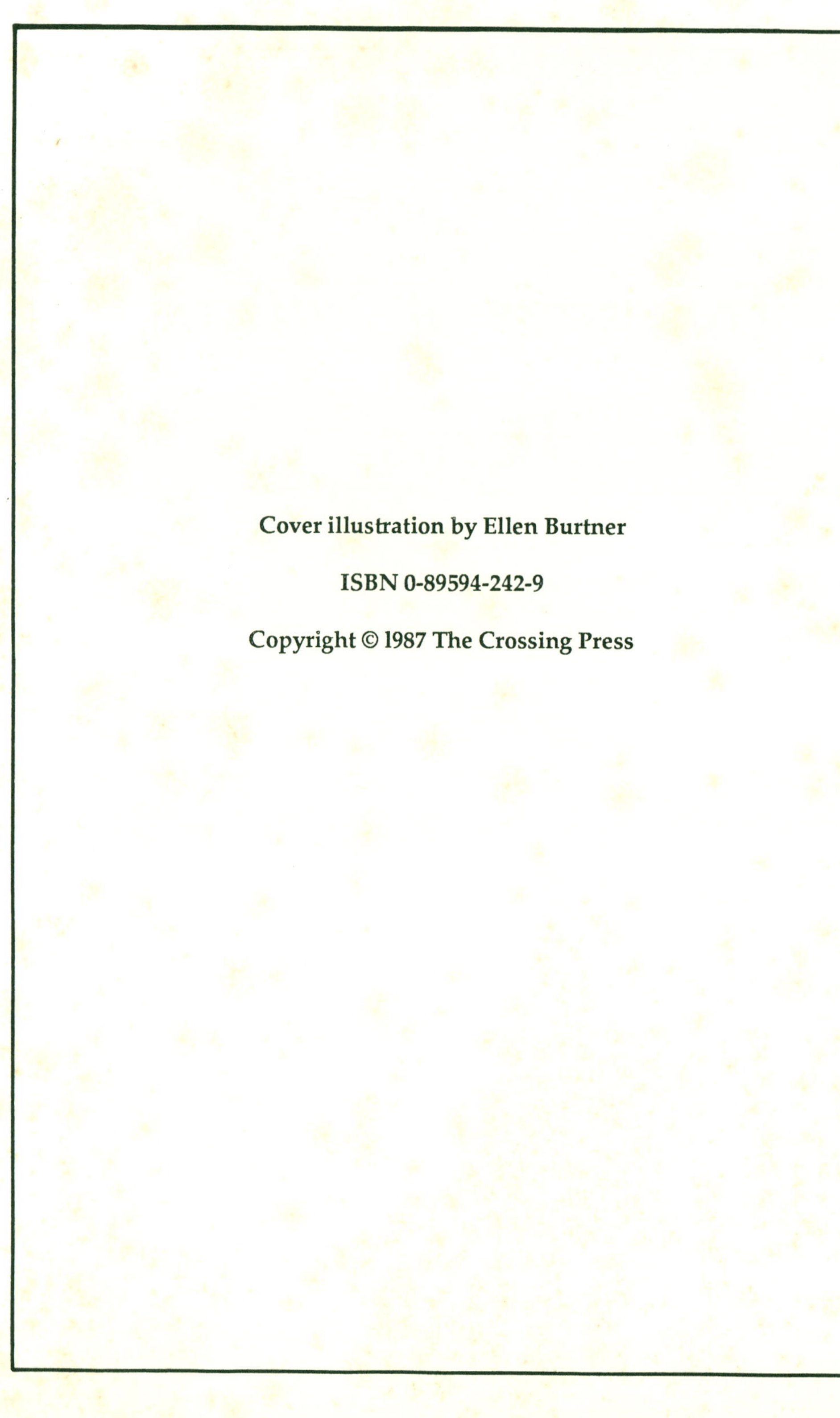

Cover illustration by Ellen Burtner

ISBN 0-89594-242-9

Welcome to the world of ferns. You can enjoy the cool, lacy fronds of ferns from all over the world while using this book as a journal or to keep records. Each fern is identified with its Latin name plus its common name when that was available. There are also choice poetic quotes to make this book a useful and beautiful treasure of nature.

—Publisher's Note

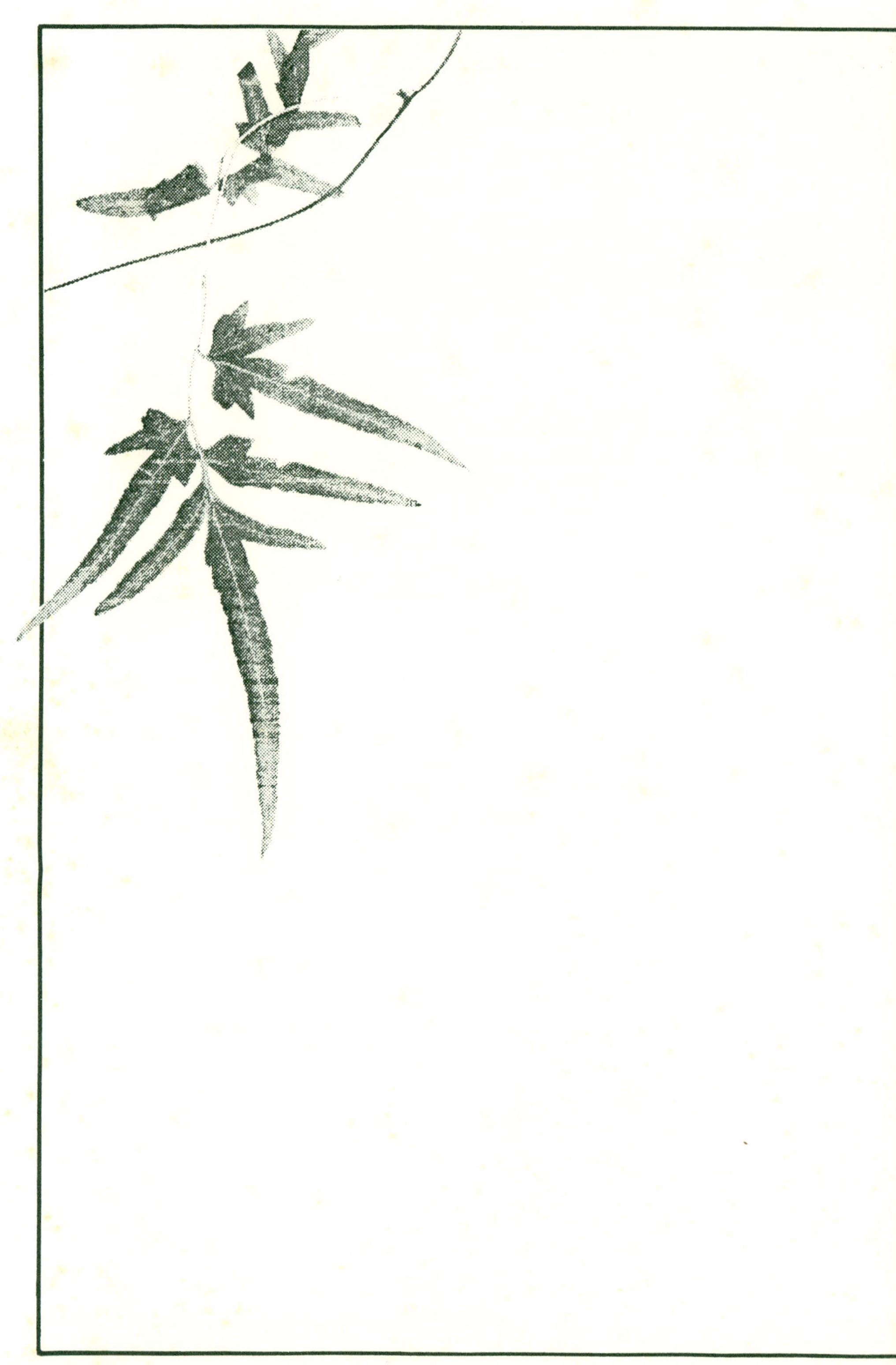

Japanese Climbing Fern—*Lygodium japonicum*

—enter the primitive world
of ferns and mosses breathing as they have
for lost millions of years.

—John Gill

I'd watched on bleak, blue days of gusty March,
The swallow hither and thither skirring low
After the flies along the river's flow

—T. C. Irwin

Maidenhair—*Adiantum diplazium*

Llavea cordifolia

Silence of woods amid green mellow lights,
And sighs of distant drizzling waterfalls

—T. C. Irwin

Polypodium, relative species

Maidenhair—*Adiantum tenerum scutum roseum*

The spring wind passes over the willows;
they are green like silk.

—Wang An-Shih

Little silver fish
pointing upstream
moving downstream
in clear quick water.
—Soseki

Trembling Brake—*Pteris tremula*

Hark, how his winds have changed their note,
And with warm whispers call thee out.
The frosts are past, the storms are gone,
And backward life at last comes on.

—Henry Vaughan

Walking Maidenhair—*Adiantum caudatum*

There is a Flower, the lesser Celandine,
that shrinks, like many more, from cold and rain;
And, the first moment that the sun may shine,
Bright as the Sun himself, 'tis out again!

—William Wordsworth

Maidenhair—*Adiantum raddianum*

O Western wind, when wilt thou blow
        That the small rain down can rain?
Christ, that my love were in my arms,
        And I in my bed again!

—Anon.

Dawn comes, spreading a white rug;
Towers, pavilions and rivers—all look alike.
All are glittering silver, like white jade.

—Su Shih

Rough Maidenhair — *Adiantum hispidulum*

There is midnight water,
waveless, windless,
the old boat's swamped
with moonlight.
—Dogen

Here is the dark tree
bare now
of leaves
But a million stars!
—Shiki

Himalayan Maidenhair—*Adiantum venustum*

The sky is all serene and mild
The sun is gleaming far away
So sweet so rich — the very child
Would feel its maker brought the May.
— John Clare

I cannot see what flowers are at my feet,
        Nor what soft incense hangs upon the boughs,
But, in enbalmed darkness, guess each sweet
        Wherewith the seasonable month endows
The grass, the thicket, and the fruit-tree wild;

—John Keats

Maidenhair—*Adiantum raddianum*

Squirrel's Foot Fern—*Davallia* species

It's summer—
And from the orchard's south brick walling
You hear the peach in the hot hush falling.
—T. C. Irwin

Earth of the vitreous pour of the full moon just tinged with blue! . . .
Far-swooping elbowed earth! Rich apple-blossomed earth!
Smile for your lover comes!

—Walt Whitman

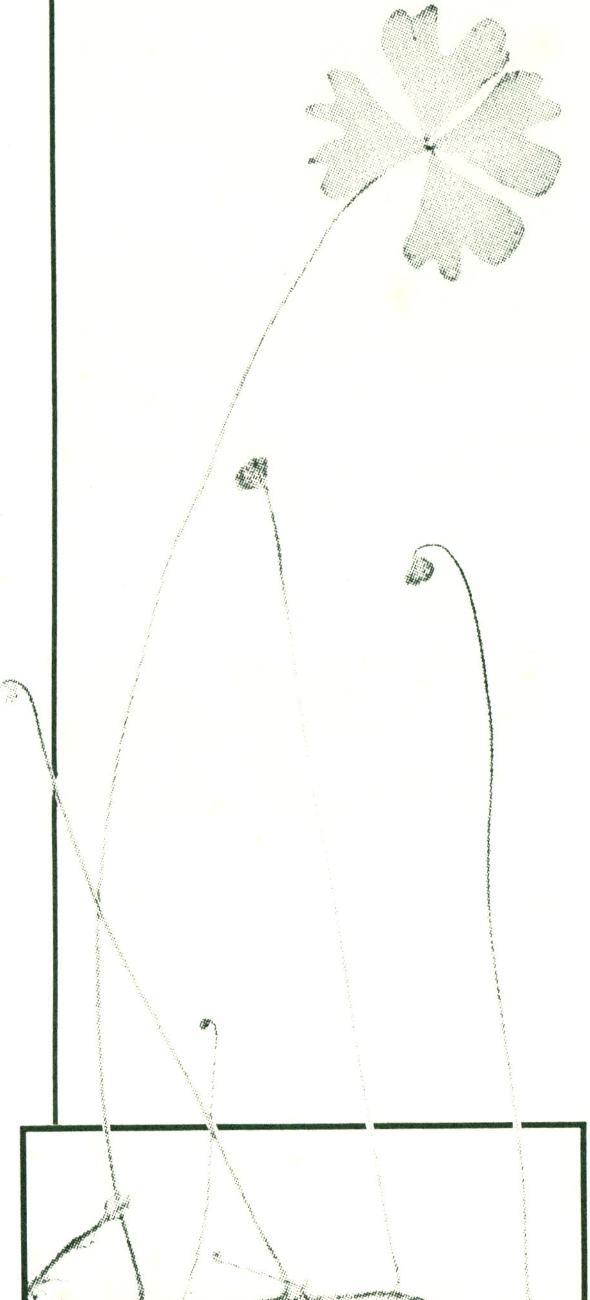

Semi-Aquatic Fern—*Marsilea* species

Thou perceivest the Flowers put
Forth their precious Odours,
And none can tell how from so small
A center comes such sweets.
—William Blake

The iris looks exactly like the one in the water.

—Matsuo Basho

Japanese Climbing Fern—*Lygodium japonicum*

Hanging Maidenhair—*Adiantum raddianum*

And what is so rare as a day in June?
Then, if ever, come perfect days;
—James Russell Lowell

One impulse from a vernal wood
May teach you more of man,
Of moral evil and of good,
Than all the sages can.
—William Wordsworth

Maidenhair—*Adiantum tenerum*

The moan of doves in immemorial elms,
And murmuring of innumerable bees.
—Alfred Tennyson

Rain is over, a pure fragrance spreads.
—ou-yang Hsiu

Maidenhair—*Adiantum diplazium*

Bear's Paw Fern—*Phlebodium (polypodium) aureum*

O bitter song
of water on stone!
Toward high Espino
under the stars.
—Antonio Machado

A Bird came down the Walk—
He did not know I saw—
He bit an Angle worm in halves
And ate the fellow, raw.
—Emily Dickinson

Maidenhair—*Adiantum raddianum*

I hear the sound of bells floating across the cold water;
Step by step, together we climb toward the cloudy peaks.
—ou-yang Hsiu

Sun at dawn wraps itself in last night's clouds.
—ou-yang Hsiu

Maidenhair—*Adiantum trapeziforme*

Glory be to God for dappled things—
For skies of couple-color as a brindled cow;
For rose-moles all in stiple upon trout that swim;
—Gerard Manley Hopkins

Spring enters the mountain village, Flowers everywhere.
Green peace, though formless, here finds its form;
Solitary smoke curls upward; men live here.

—Su Shih

chi-chirp — chi-chirp — beside the hearth
the cricket cheers the dusk with mirth.
— T. C. Irwin

A morning-glory at my window satisfies me more than
the metaphysics of books.

—Walt Whitman

Table Fern—*Pteris longifolia*

Broad Beech Fern—*Phegopteris hexagonoptera*

The south wind blows across the river;
peach flowers float on the water and fingerlings grow fat.
—Wang An-Shih

the cuckoo
repeating his cry,
how clear and cool
the color of his voice.
 —Kyogoku Tamekane

Boston—*Nephrolepis exaltata*

Maidenhair—*Adiantum pubescens*

Even if I held it
Could I touch the
Lightness of this
Butterfly?

—Buson

Hedge-crickets sing; and now with treble soft
The redbreast whistles from a garden-croft,
And gathering swallows twitter in the skies.
—John Keats

What wondrous life is this I lead!
Ripe apples drop about my head;
The luscious clusters of the vine
Upon my mouth do crush their wine . . .
—Andrew Marvell

Maidenhair—*Adiantum cunningham II*

Sweet is the lore which Nature brings;
Our meddling intellect
Misshapes the beauteous forms of things
We murder to dissect.
—William Wordsworth

Squirrel's Foot Fern—*Davallia* species

Nephrolepis biserrata

The bee hummed over the withering flowers,
And the thistle-down went on the wind.
—T. C. Irwin

Christmas Fern—*Polystichum acrostichoides*

Table Fern—*Pteris*, species

Below the blossoming sierra
the broad sea bubbles.
In my honeycomb of bees
are tiny flakes of salt.

—Antonio Machado

To grass, or leaf, or fruit, or wall,
The snail sticks close, nor fears to fall,
As if he grew there, house and all
Together.

—William Cowper

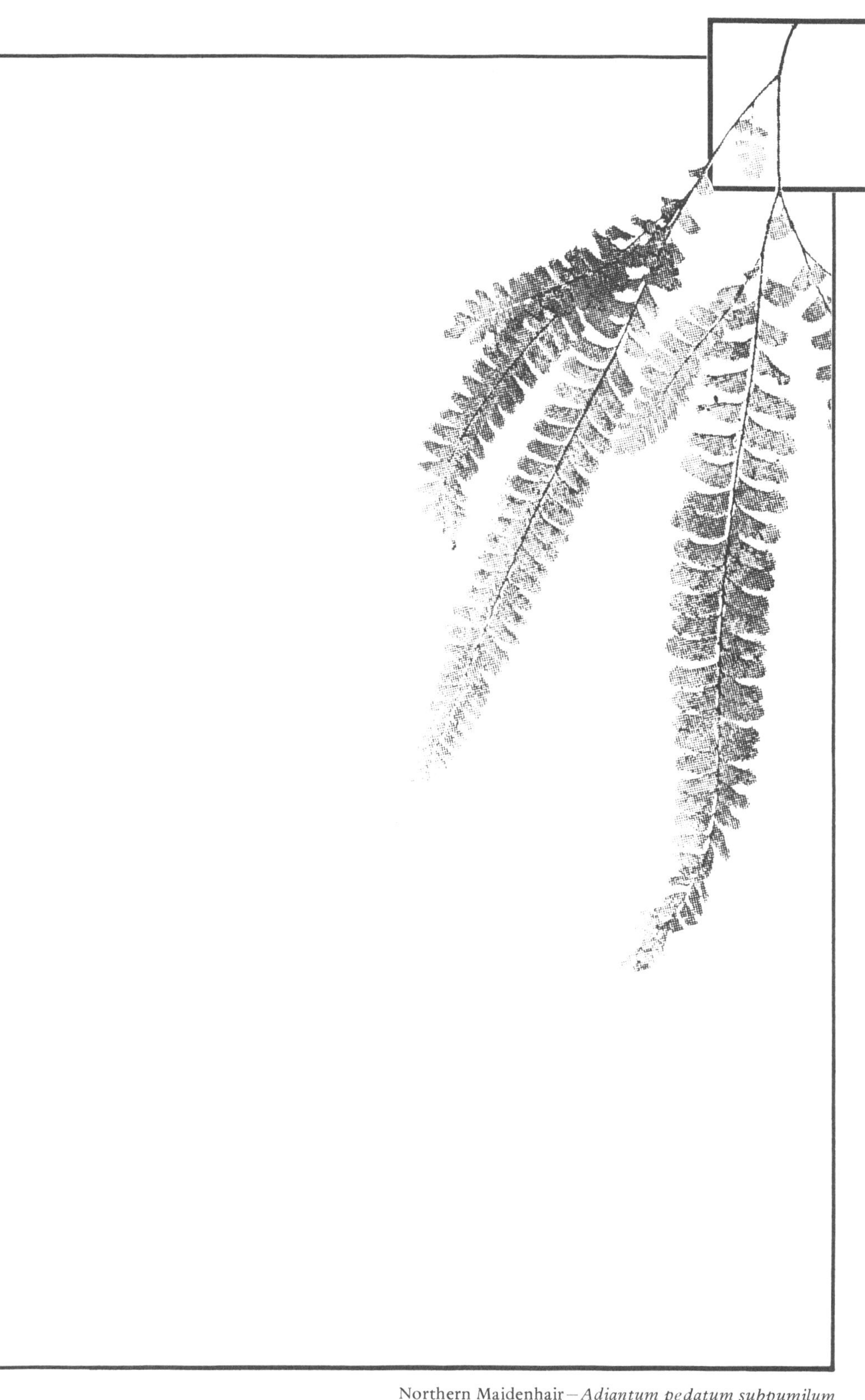

Northern Maidenhair—*Adiantum pedatum subpumilum*

Stenochlaena tenufolia

To one who has been long in city pent,
'Tis very sweet to look into the fair
And open face of heaven,—to breathe a prayer
Full in the smile of the blue firmament.

—John Keats

Love in my bosom like a bee
    Doth suck his sweet:
Now with his wings he plays with me,
    Now with his feet.

—Thomas Lodge

Tsusima Holly Fern – *Polystichum tsus-simense*

Crickets—
as the cold night
deepens into autumn
are you weakening?
your voices grow farther and farther away.
—Saigyo

Table Fern—*Pteris longifolia*

you fall asleep
to the old pond sucking its gums,
peepers' pulse
the deeper bass of frog.

—John Gill

Even a person free of passion
would understand
this sadness:
autumn evening
in a marsh where snipes fly up.
—Saigyo

Maidenhair—*Adiantum raddianum*

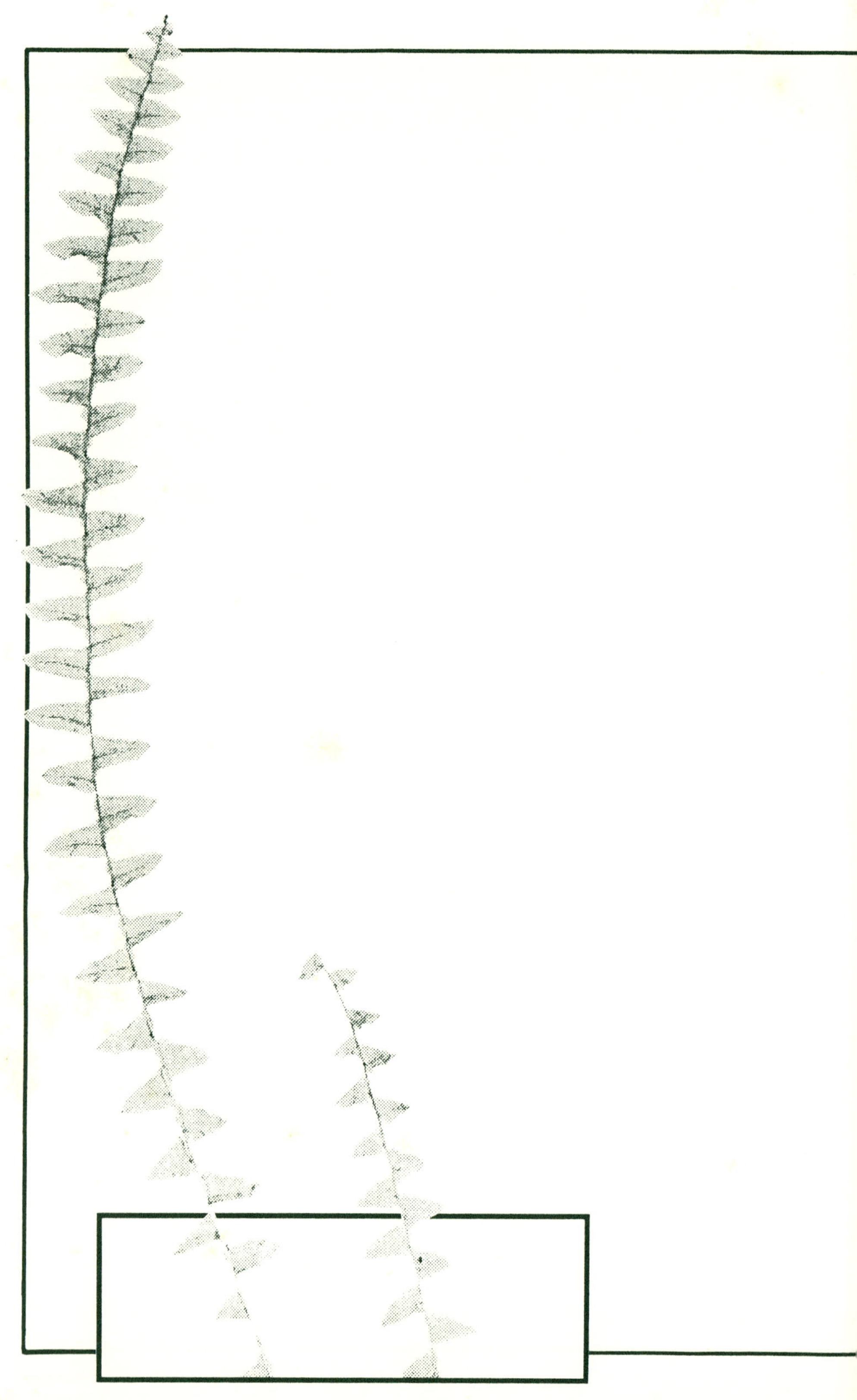

The scarlet of the maples can shake me like a cry
Of bugles going by.
And my lonely spirit thrills
To see the frosty asters like a smoke upon the hills.

—Bliss Carman

Dwarf Boston—*Nephrolepis exaltata*

Look at that stray cat
    Sleeping . . . snug
    Under the eaves
In the whistling snow.
—Taigi

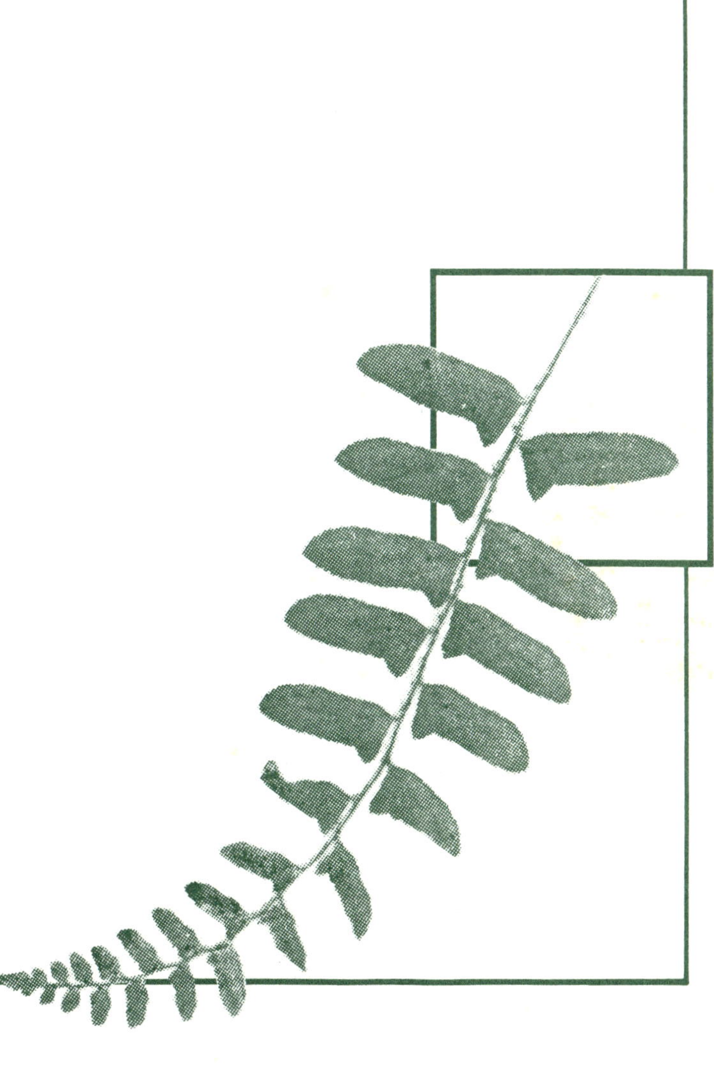

Tsusima Holly Fern—*Polystichum tsus-simense*

Through the white sierra,
the delicate snow
and wind in your face.
—Antonio Machado

Come to the creek and free the boat;
sit with your back to the mountain.
With the river birds and mountain flowers,
share my leisure.

—Wang An-Shih

Nicaraguan Maidenhair—*Adiantum concinnum*

Broad (Northern) Beech Fern—*Phegopteris hexagonoptera*

There is a pleasure in the pathless woods,
There is a rapture on the lonely shore,
There is society where none intrudes
By the deep Sea, and music in its roar.
—Lord Byron

My heart leaps up when I behold
A rainbow in the sky:
So was it when my life began;
So is it now I am a man.
—William Wordsworth

Maidenhair—*Adiantum raddianum*

I plant the pit
in my small garden
        waiting for the time
        when the tree
        will flower and bear fruit!
                —Masaoka Shiki

I must go down to the seas again,
    to the lonely sea and the sky,
And all I ask is a tall ship and a star to steer her by.
—John Masefield

Sensitive Fern—*Onoclea sensibilis*

Green Cliff Brake—*Pellaea viridis*

Hark, where my blossomed pear-tree in the hedge
Leans to the fields and scatters on the clover
Blossoms and dewdrops—at the bent-spray's edge—
—Robert Browning

Where is the pride of Summer—the green prime—
the many, many leaves all twinkling?—Three
On the mossed elm; three on the naked lime
Trembling,—and one upon the old oak tree!

—Thomas Hood

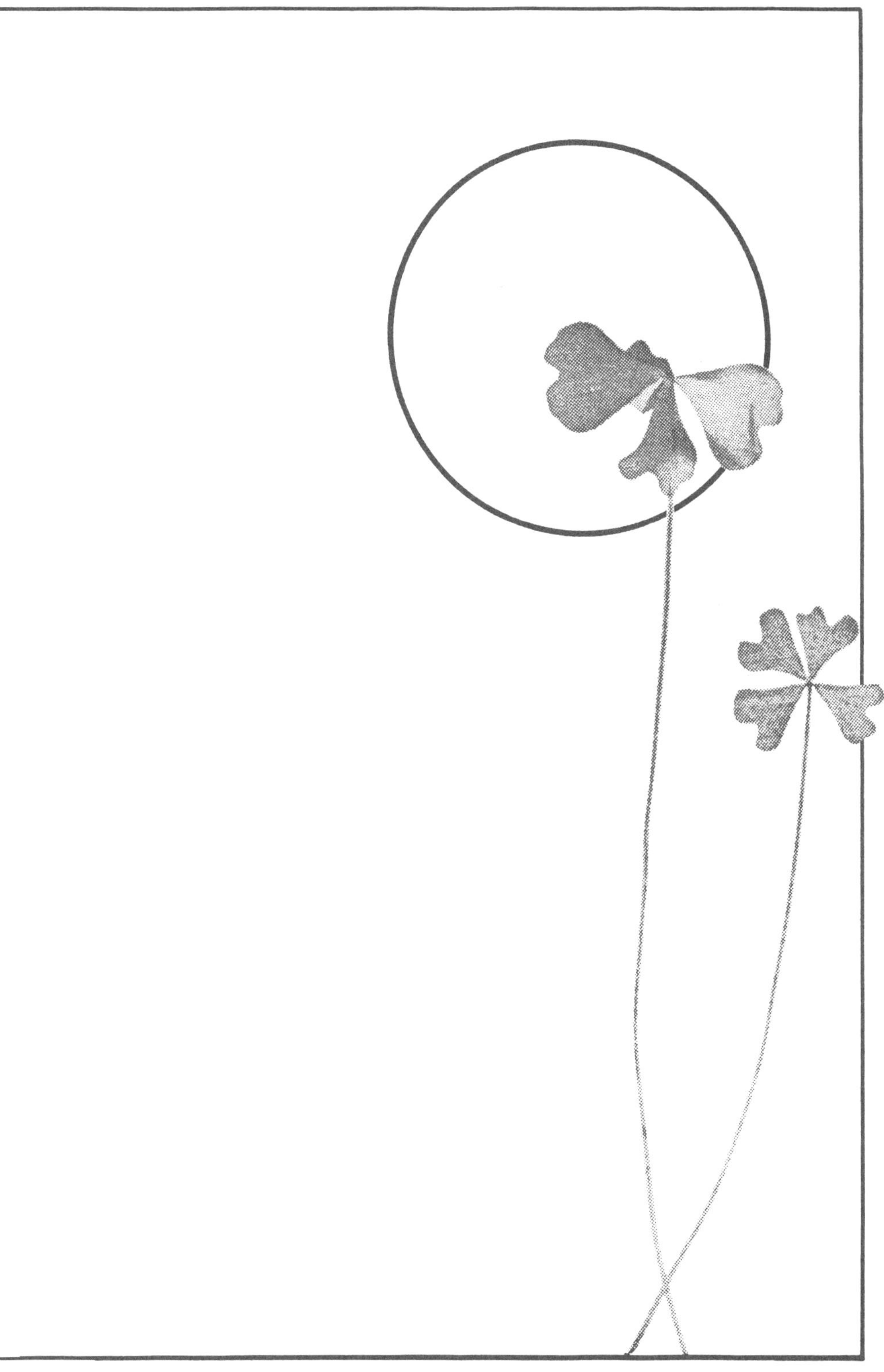

Knight's Polypody—*Polypodium subauriculatum*

The insect world amid the suns and dews
Awake and hum their tiny songs anew,
And climb the totter-grass and blossom's stem
As huge in size as mighty oaks to them.
—John Clare

notice how the crows uplift
and drift as they beat
across the snow-stubbled field.
—John Gill

Leather Fern—*Rumohra adiantiformis*

In May, when sea-winds pierced our solitudes,
I found the fresh Rhodora in the woods,
Spreading its leafless blooms in the damp nook,
To please the desert and the sluggish brook.

—Ralph Waldo Emerson

I'll tell you how the Sun rose—
A Ribbon at a time—
the Steeples swam in Amethyst—
the news, like Squirrels, ran—
the Hills untied their Bonnets—
the Bobolinks—began.

—Emily Dickinson

Japanese Climbing Fern—*Lygodium japonicum*

Maidenhair—*Adiantum diplazium*

And I know . . . that a kelson of the creation is love;
And limitless are leaves stiff or drooping in the fields,
And brown ants in the little wells beneath them,
And mossy scabs of the wormfence, and heaped stones,
and elder and mullen and pokeweed.

—Walt Whitman

From the very beginning
All things are in bliss—
Here's spring with hundreds of blossoms,
A yellow warbler singing in the willows.
—Anon.

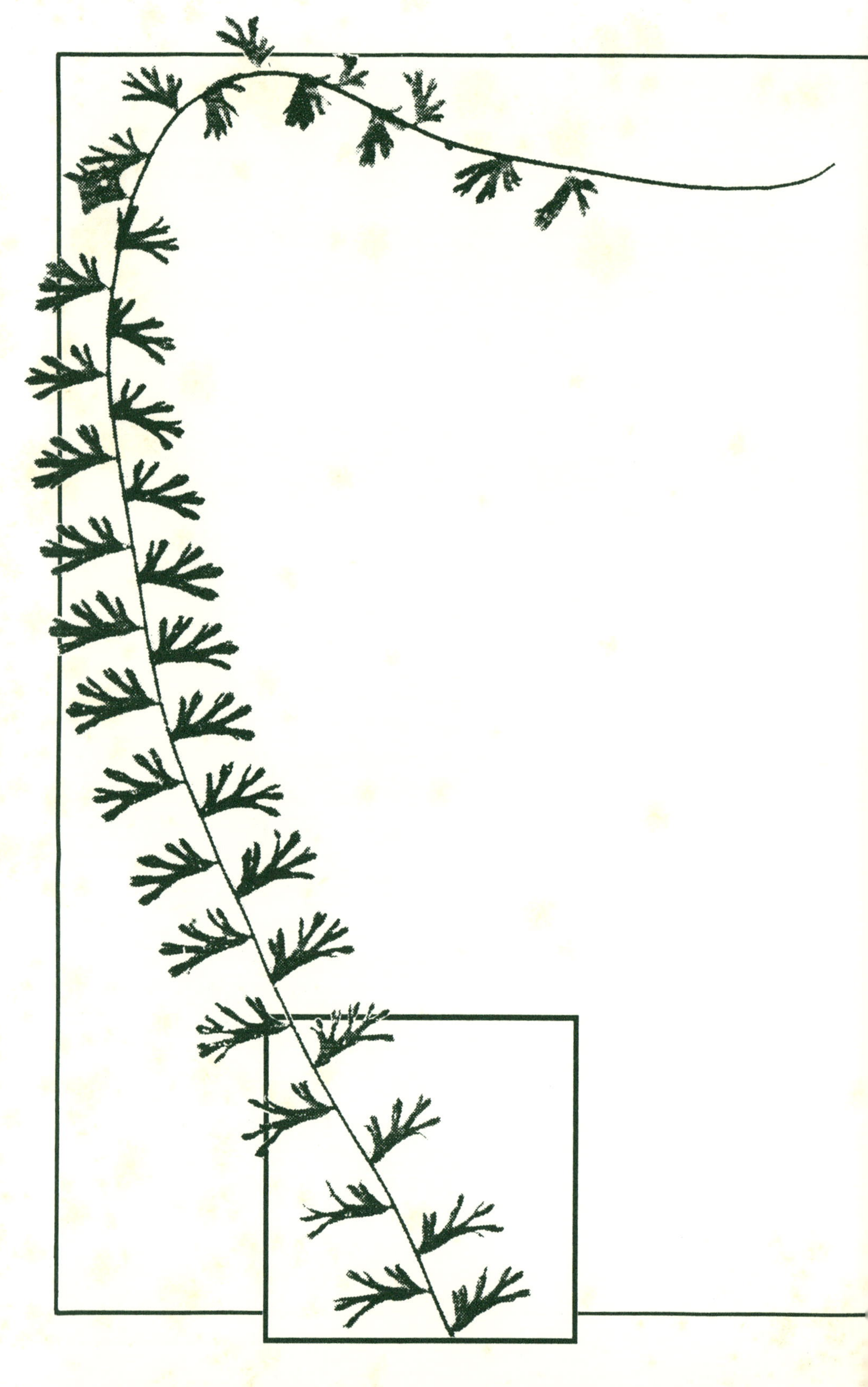

To see a world in a grain of sand
And a Heaven in a wild flower,
Hold Infinity in the palm of your hand
And Eternity in an hour.
—William Blake

Walking Maidenhair—*Adiantum caudatum*